BEASTS AND BIRDS

Poems and Pictures of North American Wildlife

Maisy Moonbeam

MPM Publishing Co. (Toronto, Canada)

2023

Table of Contents

The Forest

In the North American woods, so wild and grand,
Lies a world that's waiting, just waiting to expand.
Where animals roam, and the trees reach high,
It's a place of wonder, a place to glorify.

So many creatures are roaming freely there,
All unique, and each with special flair.
From deer and bears to birds with wide wings,
They all live together and roar or sing.

The rustling leaves, the swaying trees,
Create a tune that will enchant you with ease.
A world of magic, where you fulfill your dreams,
Anything can happen, and nothing is what is seems.

So, let's go, a wonderful journey we are going to take,
To explore the forest and the world that it has made.
You can wander and learn, your mind runs wild and free,
And you will discover a place where you crave to be.

Let's walk on meadows among the trees to find
Wonders of nature, marvelous and one of a kind.
And while we roam through the North American woods,
The magic of nature will fill your heart and your moods.

The forest will teach you how to think and care
For creatures and trees, in a place that all of us share.
We all are part of a cycle that keeps our world strong,
And helps us to learn, what is good and what is wrong.

Fox

Here we meet the fox, so quick and so sly,
His fur as red as the sunrise in the sky,
Eyes piercing and sharp, his nose so keen,
He roamed the forests through the meadows green.

He ate rabbits and birds, but never got into strife,
For he was clever and stealthy all of his life,
Waiving bushy tail that looked like a flag,
He disappeared under the bushes with a wag.

Bear

Here is the big and furry bear who is strong and bold.
His roar echoes in the woods with strength untold.
He roams the mountains, and the forests wide,
With his big, black nose sniffing site after site.

He eats honey and berries, and sometimes fish too,
But mostly he sleeps, and that is what all bears do,
So, if you see him, from a distance you can say hello,
He's just a big softie, you'll surely know.

Wolf

In the woods, day or night, everyone hears the wolf's howl,
So mournful and loud, it can send shivers down your soul,
Roaming the forests with a pack of other wolves by his side,
He is a hunter so skilled that no one from him can hide.

He eats birds and rabbits, and sometimes a deer,
And when the moon is full, his voice is all you can hear,
So if you feel his howl is near, don't be too afraid,
It's just a wolf, singing to his pack in the shade.

Bald Eagle

With wings that soar, so proud and bold,
The Bald Eagle flies, with a heart of gold,
His white head shines in the sky so blue,
He is a symbol, of our nation true.

He scans the land with eyes as sharp as steel,
To catch the prey below, moving in the field.
So let him soar high and free, and give a home
To this bird of freedom that deserves a throne.

Bobcat

There's a small, wild cat, so gracious and neat,
With spots as black as coal, and fur as soft as wheat,
You can find him in the woods, and in mountains high,
And watch him pounce on his prey, with a sudden cry.

He eats mice and rabbits, and sometimes a bird,
Once done with his meal, he'll lick his whiskers and purr,
So if you see him, be quiet and still,
And you might catch a glimpse of this forest thrill.

Raven

With a glossy coat, and a voice so hoarse,
The Raven, is a bird with a rare force,
He caws and croaks, with a call so bold,
And his eyes can spark with a gleam so cold.

18

Mischief has filled his heart, his mind is always wise,
A bird of riddles, that always brings surprise,
A tree with sturdy twigs is all he needs as his place,
So let this clever bird live safely in his forest space.

Squirrel

There's a tiny creature, with a bushy tail,
And fur as soft as a downy quail,
He jumps from tree to tree, with a skippy skip,
And gathers acorns, with a busy dip.

His cheeks are plump, with a nut or two,
And his eyes are bright, with a twinkle that's true,
So, if you see him, don't be too rough,
For he's just a little guy, trying to be tough.

Barred Owl

With a call so soft, and eyes so bright,
The Barred Owl is calling in the night.
He hoots and hollers, and his voice is sweet,
And his eyes gleam, with a moonlit beat.

And when he starts his flight, the flutter is so light,
He glides through air over grass, with a grace so right,
He boldly guards his dark enchanted space,
For this bird of beauty, needs his cozy place.

Deer

Behold the graceful deer, with antlers tall and fine,
In the meadows and forests, is where he roams and dines,
He eats leaves and grass, and sometimes some bark,
And when he's scared, he'll run with a leap in the dark.

His big gentle eyes look at you among the trees,
And his coat is as soft as a summertime breeze,
So if you see him, don't be too shy,
Just watch him for a while, and let him roam by.

Raccoon

He looks like a bandit at night, with his masked face,
And fur as soft as velvet embrace,
He rummages through the trash, with a curious snout,
And his little hands always moving in and out.

26

He eats anything, from crumbs to even cream,
And washes it down, with a drink from a stream,
And he dips his face in the water shiny and cold,
He is just the friendly raccoon with a heart of gold.

Great Blue Heron

With a long neck, and legs so straight,
The Great Blue Heron, is a sight that's great,
Standing still in the shallowest streams,
He eyes the flowing water's gleam.

28

And when he strikes, he's quick and sure,
With a lightning-fast beak, that's strong and pure,
So let him live in peace and quiet grace,
For this bird of beauty deserves a greeny place.

Moose

Here comes the giant of the woods, with antlers grand,
And a coat as brown as the autumn land,
He munches on leaves and twigs, and even chews a shrub,
And looks at you with eyes so big and so gentle and snug.

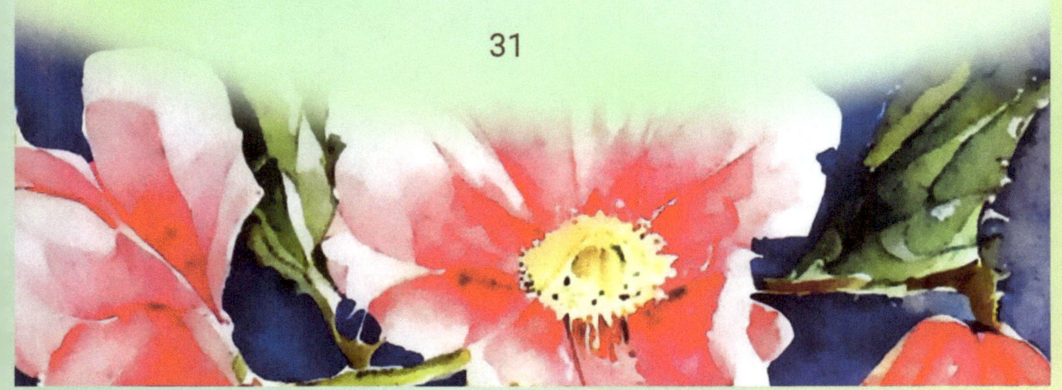

The moose walks in the forest, with calm and stately pace,
And his big, warm heart, is full of gentle grace,
For he's just a big guy, wandering by
Under the puffy clouds and the blue sky.

Coyote

With fur as gray as a winter's sky, and a voice so sharp,
The coyote, roams the wild when it is light or dark,
He growls and howls, and hides behind a shrub or tree,
And his eyes gleam, for his soul is so wild and free.

And when he hunts, with a skill unmatched,
He chases his prey, and it can't escape his catch,
Let's leave him wander the woods in his chosen space,
For the cunning coyote deserves a warm place.

Osprey

With wings stretched wide, and stance so bold,
The Osprey soars high in heat or cold,
He catches prey, diving from above,
And his talons grip, with strength so rough.

34

And when he flies high above with a cry so clear,
His beauty shines, in the sky so sheer.
Let him soar to the clouds called his home,
For this bird of freedom, deserves a throne.

35

Beaver

There's a builder in the pond, with a busy mind,
And a tail that slaps, but he is calm and kind,
He chews down trees, and builds a dam,
And makes a lodge that's cozy like a warm ham.

36

He eats bark and leaves, and sometimes a twig,
And his little eyes twinkle, like a fire lit,
So if you see him, don't be too rough,
For he's just a little guy, trying to be tough.

Chipmunk

Chipmunks, oh Chipmunks, with stripes on their back,
Their little legs scamper to pick snack after snack.
With cheeks as plump as a harvest moon,
They gather acorns, in the afternoon.

They nibble on seeds, and crunch on a nut,
And burrow their homes, with a little dirt-tut.
So if you see one, don't be too shy,
Just smile and wave, as they scamper by.

Great Horned Owl

His hoot is so deep, and the eyes are so bright.
The Great Horned Owl, calls in the night,
He swivels his head, with a grace to admire,
And his eyes gleam, like hearths with bright fire.

And when he takes flight, with a flutter so light,
He glides through the air, with a grace so right,
So let's protect him, and give him his space,
For this bird of wonder needs a wonderful place.

Wild Turkey

With feathers plump, and a strut so grand,
The Wild Turkey in a shady meadow stands,
He struts his stuff every time he wants to shine,
His gobble is grand and always looks fine.

And when he takes flight, with a flutter so light,
He soars up to the skies with a wonderful might,
And when he strolls in the grass among the trees,
This is the only home that he likes and needs.

Peregrine Falcon

With wings that are wide, he soars, swift and strong,
The Peregrine Falcon, speeds along,
High in the sky, he hunts with deadly grace,
And his talons strike, with a fatal pace.

A skillful hunter, with eyes so keen and neat,
He's a bird of prey, that cannot be beat.
So let us look at him, admiring his stance,
For this courageous bird deserves his chance.

Wood Stork

With a bald head, and a beak so long,
The Wood Stork, a bird so proud and strong,
He wades through water under sky so blue,
And looks for prey, to his hunting nature true.

And when he finds his prey, with a dive so deep,
His beak snaps shut, with a skill to keep,
So let's protect him in his sawgrass home,
And leave this bird of wonder free to roam.

47

www.ingramcontent.com/pod-product-compliance
Lightning Source LLC
Chambersburg PA
CBHW041225050726
47599CB00001B/81